HUMAN RIGHTS
JOURNALISM

INVESTIGATIVE JOURNALISM THAT INSPIRED CHANGE

DIANE DAKERS

Crabtree Publishing Company

www.crabtreebooks.com

Author: Diane Dakers

Series research and development:
Janine Deschenes and Reagan Miller

Editorial director: Kathy Middleton

Editor: Janine Deschenes

Proofreaders: Wendy Scavuzzo, Melissa Boyce

Design and photo research:
Katherine Berti

Print and production coordinator:
Katherine Berti

Images:

AP Images: Dita Alangkara: p. 18
features.weather.com
    Screen Shot 2018-07-11 at 1.15.47 PM: p. 41
Istockphoto
    Joel Carillet: p. 38
    RichLegg: p. 27 (top)
Shutterstock
    Aldelo Piomica: p. 19
    Anton Ivanov: p. 37
    Aung Myat: p. 14
    CervelliInFuga: front cover (newspapers)
    chrisdorney: p. 13 (bottom)
    diyben: p. 15 (bottom left)
    Elnur: p. 32 (center right)
    GeorginaCaptures: p. 13 (top)
    Joseph Sorrentino: p. 40 (top left)
    Lawrey: p. 1 (top right), 6 (bottom right)
    Pavel Svoboda Photography: p. 4 (bottom)
    REDPIXEL.PL: p. 11 (bottom left)
    Rob Crandall: front cover (center left)
    Tropical studio: p. 15 (center)
    Watchares Hansawek: p. 17
Thinkstock Photos: Tigercat_LPG: front cover (top left)
www.ap.org
    Screen Shot 2018-07-10 at 3.18.26 PM: p. 21 (bottom right)
www.publicintegrity.org
    Screen Shot 2018-07-11 at 10.29.58 AM: p. 33 (top)
www.pulitzer.org
    Screen Shot 2018-07-10 at 3.27.28 PM: p. 23
    Screen Shot 2018-07-11 at 10.38.58 AM: p. 33 (bottom right)
All other images by Shutterstock

Library and Archives Canada Cataloguing in Publication

Dakers, Diane, author
        Human rights journalism / Diane Dakers.

(Investigative journalism that inspired change)
Includes bibliographical references and index.
Issued in print and electronic formats.
ISBN 978-0-7787-5351-3 (hardcover).--
ISBN 978-0-7787-5364-3 (softcover).--
ISBN 978-1-4271-2198-1 (HTML)

        1. Human rights--Press coverage--Juvenile literature.
2. Human rights--Press coverage--Case studies--Juvenile literature.
3. Human rights in mass media--Juvenile literature. I. Title.

P96.H85D35 2018   j070.4'49323   C2018-905447-6
                                                                                C2018-905448-4

Library of Congress Cataloging-in-Publication Data

Available at the Library of Congress

Crabtree Publishing Company

www.crabtreebooks.com   1-800-387-7650

Printed in the U.S.A./122018/CG20181005

**Published
in Canada**
Crabtree Publishing
616 Welland Ave.
St. Catharines, Ontario
L2M 5V6

**Published in the
United States**
Crabtree Publishing
PMB 59051
350 Fifth Avenue, 59th Floor
New York, New York 10118

**Published in the
United Kingdom**
Crabtree Publishing
Maritime House
Basin Road North, Hove
BN41 1WR

**Published
in Australia**
Crabtree Publishing
3 Charles Street
Coburg North
VIC 3058

CONTENTS

INVESTIGATING HUMAN RIGHTS

Investigative journalists are reporters who write in-depth, focused stories on particular topics and issues.

Most people enjoy eating a variety of foods. Some of those foods are grown or produced close to home. Other foods are not available from nearby farms or manufacturers. In those cases, food is **imported**, or brought in, from faraway places. Although imported foods add variety to our meals, we can't always know how those foods are produced, gathered, or farmed.

When we buy imported foods, we trust that the people, animals, and environment that provide our food are treated **ethically**. For example, we trust that the cows that produce our dairy products are not treated badly by farmers. We trust that **fertilizers** used to grow fruits and vegetables do not harm people or the environment. We trust that the people who farm or gather our food are paid a fair wage and are not **abused** or **exploited**. Unfortunately, this is not always the case.

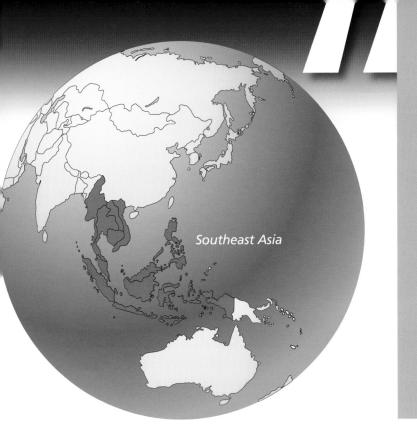

Southeast Asia

In 2015, a group of reporters uncovered a shocking case of abuse in an **industry** that supplies much of the world with a common type of food—fish and seafood. The reporters discovered that thousands of men from Southeast Asian nations were forced to catch and process seafood in **inhumane** conditions on Thai fishing boats. Some had boarded the fishing boats willingly, thinking they would make money to support their families. Others had been tricked, drugged, or kidnapped, and sold to fish boat captains.

After they boarded the ships, the men realized they were trapped. They had almost no food or clean water. They earned very little money. That's because the lower the wages the boat owners paid the workers, the more money the owners earned when they sold the fish. The workers could not leave the ships. If they tried, they would be whipped or locked in cages. Some were killed. Others chose to kill themselves to escape the misery. These men were slaves to the fishing industry. Much of the fish these slaves caught ended up in North American and European supermarkets and restaurants.

For two years, four reporters from Associated Press (AP) followed this story. They wanted the world to know about the horrors of the Southeast Asian fishing industry. They put themselves at great risk to do so— but they were determined that the story of seafood slaves be told.

RESEARCHING, REVIEWING, REPORTING

The reporters who told the story of the seafood slaves aren't **conventional** reporters. They are investigative journalists.

Unlike daily newspaper, television, or online reporters, investigative journalists might take months, or even years, to produce a finished report. That's because their stories involve greater depths of research, interviewing, and fact-checking than daily journalism stories do.

Conventional journalism often stems from information provided by others—police, governments, or businesses, for example. Based on this information, reporters read, research, and interview people in the know. They answer the important questions—especially the 5Ws.

They look into, and report on, all sides of the story. They may write **follow-ups**, or updates, later. But typically, the story comes together fairly quickly and results in a short report.

A piece of investigative journalism, on the other hand, often stems from reporters' curiosity, personal experiences, or even intuition. It is a time-consuming, team effort.

An investigative journalist finds stories in all kinds of places. It might be a document that raises more questions than it answers. It might be a tip, or a secret file provided by a source the reporter trusts. A reporter might overhear a conversation that prompts him or her to dig into a subject. Often, an investigative journalism project starts with an observation, a question that arises out of another news story, or a hunch that something isn't quite right.

A DEFINITION AND AN EXPLANATION

The **United Nations** defines investigative journalism as "the unveiling of matters that are **concealed** either deliberately by someone in a position of power, or accidentally, behind a **chaotic** mass of facts and circumstances—and the analysis and exposure of all relevant facts to the public."

Investigative journalists therefore uncover, research, and report stories that were previously hidden. These stories might have been hidden on purpose, or they were just buried so deep in documents, data, and details that nobody had dug them up before.

KNOWING THE DIFFERENCE

Different people and organizations define investigative journalism in different ways. However, most agree that it differs from conventional reporting in a number of areas:

INVESTIGATIVE JOURNALISM

- Reporter is **proactive**, takes initiative to find original stories
- Projects are long-term, requiring in-depth research
- Goal of reporter is to question
- Stories expose issues surrounded in secrecy or silence
- Stories often lead to social change

CONVENTIONAL JOURNALISM

- Reporter reacts to information provided by **sources** such as police, governments, or businesses
- Stories are short-term and present news and events of the day
- Goal of reporter is to inform
- Presents the facts of the world as it is, without questioning them

Once the investigative reporter has a story idea, he or she comes up with questions to be answered, and a plan to answer those questions. This might involve studying documents that have never been read before, or finding people who have knowledge of the subject in question. Often, an investigation also involves digging through stacks of documents and analyzing numbers and other data. This part of the job can be time-consuming and dull.

Investigative journalism projects involve a variety of tasks that require a variety of expertise. Because of this, investigative journalism projects are usually team efforts. The teams might include reporters, editors, data analysts, photographers, videographers, and fact-checkers.

Before an investigative journalist releases a story to the public, he or she must be absolutely certain every detail is correct. Like a lawyer in court, an investigative journalist has to provide evidence to prove that a story is true. The journalist must also follow laws and ethical standards to protect people's privacy and reputations.

The goal of investigative journalism is to look beyond the information already known by the public. It's about asking tough questions and finding the truth.

Investigative journalism projects might reveal wrongdoing or draw attention to important issues that have an impact on humanity. They often reveal details that have been hidden from the public—sometimes on purpose, sometimes simply because nobody had ever looked for the information before.

Because investigative journalists dig deeper and uncover previously hidden information, their work often leads to change within a community, a nation, or the world.

ROLES AND RESPONSIBILITIES

From interviews to video recordings, journalists use a variety of techniques to gather the information they need. But no matter how they gather information, they must follow certain laws and codes of ethics when they are on the job.

Laws control such things as when and where a reporter can take photos or use a recording device. Other laws ensure that a reporter doesn't make false statements that might damage a person's or a business's reputation. More laws make sure reporters don't publish material they don't have permission to use.

Codes of ethics are guidelines journalists follow while conducting their work. Different organizations have different guidelines for their staff. Generally, though, codes of ethics describe appropriate and inappropriate behavior. They also outline expectations of truth, accuracy, fairness, and **objectivity** in a reporter's work.

REPORTING ON RIGHTS

Investigative journalists are not **activists**. In the stories they publish, they may give facts about wrongdoing or identify a need for change, but they don't **protest** or actively push for change. However, they do have the power to make a difference in the world.

Through observation, research, and commitment to accurate reporting, they expose truths. Sometimes, certain people don't want these truths told. That means some investigative journalists—including those who told the seafood slavery story—take great personal risks to focus the world's attention on these issues.

Almost any topic can be the subject of an investigative journalism project—including the environment, sports, health, politics, business, and in the case of this book, human rights.

In recent years, investigative journalists around the world have covered such human rights topics as discrimination against students on the **LGBTQ spectrum**, the ill treatment of women in several countries, unsafe labor practices, and abuse of **migrant workers** and refugees.

This book focuses on three specific investigative journalism projects related to human rights: a story about miners with lung disease who were denied health benefits; a report about child labor on coffee **plantations** in Mexico; and the article about slavery in the seafood industry.

The story about the miners stemmed from a previous project on which the reporter had worked. The journalists on the coffee story happened to see children working on farms as they drove by. They knew they had to investigate. The reporters on the seafood story weren't the first to try to report on the issue—they simply refused to give up where other journalists had failed.

All three groups of investigative journalists stepped in to document—and raise public awareness about—the ill treatment of their fellow human beings.

SOURCING SOURCES

All reporters rely on sources to provide information. Examples of sources are documents, news stories, books, videos, and social media posts. A source can also be a person who has information a journalist needs.

Because reporters can't be everywhere at once, they often rely on other people, or sources, to tell them what they've seen, heard, or witnessed. Sources often provide tips to point a reporter in the direction of a news story.

Journalists spend years building relationships with sources. They get to know people in their neighborhoods and cities, people who are experts in certain fields, and workers in government offices, police departments, and other official areas. The goal is to get to know people they can trust to provide reliable information.

Sources who provide accurate material on many occasions earn the trust of reporters. Even if sources have proved to be reliable in the past, though, a journalist must always double-check new information they provide before publishing it.

"SEAFOOD FROM SLAVES"

WHO	Thai seafood companies
WHAT	Enslaved thousands of men
WHEN	Reported in 2016
WHERE	Southeast Asia
WHY	For **profit**
HOW	Tricked men into working on fish boat; workers were beaten, trapped, and starved

Having lived and worked in Southeast Asia for more than a decade, AP reporter Robin McDowell was aware of the rumors. She'd heard that Thai fishing companies were abusing their workers and forcing them to work against their will. "For those of us living in Southeast Asia, this story was really an open secret," she said. "We all knew that the Thai fishing industry was using slaves and forced labor, but proving it was another matter."

Journalists cannot publish stories based on rumors. They have to prove a story is true before reporting it to the public. That means conducting a thorough investigation, providing evidence, and finding witnesses that can confirm that the activity in question is taking place. They may also try to witness the activity for themselves.

Over the years, a number of investigative reporters in Southeast Asia had tried to find evidence to prove the slavery rumors were true. But the fishing companies always stayed one step ahead of the journalists. They worked hard to cover up their wrongdoing.

In December 2013, another AP reporter, Margie Mason, received a tip related to the seafood slavery rumors. A source told her that a large number of **Burmese** fishermen, working for Thai fishing companies, were stranded in Indonesia. "We decided that was the place to look," said Margie, who was based in Jakarta, Indonesia.

Fishing is a huge money-maker in Southeast Asia. However, as the reporters found, many poor men there are **vulnerable** to being mistreated, because they need the money from fishing to survive.

At that point, she and Robin joined forces for the investigation. They had both worked in the region for years. They were well connected, with many sources throughout Southeast Asia. They believed one of these sources would know someone, or something, that might lead them to the evidence they needed.

They knew it would take a lot of time and money to investigate slavery in the fishing industry. They knew it would be nearly impossible to prove. At the same time, they felt they had a responsibility to do their best to uncover the abuse, and to help the mistreated men.

NEWS FOR THE WORLD

The reporters on the Seafood Slavery series work for Associated Press (AP), which is the largest international news agency in the world. Based in New York City, it has 263 news offices in 106 countries. AP is also the oldest English-language news agency in the world.

AP publishes stories, videos, and photos on its website. It also distributes those stories to thousands of news outlets, or companies, around the world.

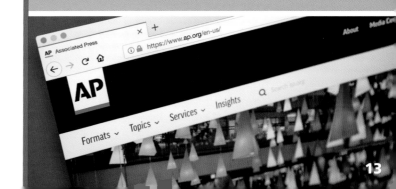

Most investigative journalists share a commitment to uncovering the truth and a drive to right the world's wrongs. Patience and focus are other common qualities of investigative journalists.

Margie and Robin displayed all these qualities over the next two years. That's how long it took them—and two other AP reporters—to pull together the proof they needed to publish the seafood slavery story.

To gather evidence, these reporters used almost every investigative journalism technique in the book—interviews, hidden cameras, **satellite** technology, personal observation, Internet research, **stakeouts**, travel to risky locations, and **networking**. And in many cases, the reporters uncovered information simply by being in the right place at the right time.

Yangon is the largest city in Myanmar.

WHAT'S IN A NAME?

At the time of the Seafood Slavery stories, Associated Press reporter Robin McDowell lived in Yangon, Myanmar. Or was that Rangoon, Burma?

In 1989, for political reasons, the nation that had for centuries been called Burma changed its name to Myanmar.

Since then, most people haven't been sure what to call this Southeast Asian country. In fact, both names are used by people who live there. "Myanmar" is more formal, and is used in ceremonial, official, and other published documents. "Burma" is the less formal name often used by locals. Burmese fishermen were some of the people being enslaved by Thai fishing companies in Indonesia.

Despite its decline after Margie and Robin's story broke, human rights abuses still occur in the Thai fishing industry. The organization Human Rights Watch explains that the Thailand government has not taken the necessary steps to enforce, or carry out, laws against abuse and slavery.

FISHING FOR PROFITS

Until 2015, when the Associated Press published its Seafood Slavery series, Thailand was the world's third-largest seafood **exporter**.

At the time, the Thai fishing industry earned about $7 billion a year. Because there was so much money to be made, fish boats flocked to the oceans in the area. Eventually, the area was overfished. That meant boats had to travel further and further from shore to keep catching. Eventually, some Thai fishing companies began working illegally in foreign waters.

Meanwhile, the oceans around Indonesia teemed with seafood. Many Thai fishing boats pretended they were Indonesian so they could fish there. They faked paperwork for the boats and workers, flew Indonesian flags, and sailed in and out of Indonesian villages. They enslaved poverty-stricken men who were desperate for jobs.

After the Associated Press exposed this human rights abuse, Thailand's fishing industry suffered. It is no longer among the world's top seafood exporters.

Men who were desperate to make money to survive were tricked into slavery on fishing boats.

"SLAVE ISLAND"

Courage and risk-taking are common qualities in investigative journalists—and they are qualities Robin and Margie displayed in covering this story. Their investigation eventually led them to dangerous places, people, and situations. But it started out quite simply.

When they agreed to launch the seafood slavery investigation, Robin and Margie didn't have a solid starting point. All they had were rumors and a tip that there may be Burmese slaves in Indonesia. They didn't let this lack of information discourage them. Instead, they spent the next year networking, following leads, and searching the Internet to find out where in Indonesia the Burmese workers might be.

Their search eventually led them to the remote, or isolated, island town of Benjina. No public records, documents, or online sources contained information about the people working there—the fishing companies had made sure of that. The only way the reporters could find out if Burmese workers were trapped on the island was to go there.

Robin traveled to the island with a photographer and videographer from Associated Press, who would record the evidence they uncovered there. Robin knew that if there were slaves in Benjina, the people who had captured them wouldn't want the world to know about it. If they suspected Robin was looking into slavery, she knew they would try and stop her—meaning she and her colleagues would be in danger.

The island town of Benjina is inaccessible for much of the year because of stormy seas. It has no roads, electricity, or Internet access.

Because of this, the AP team lied to officials about what they were investigating in Benjina. "We said we were doing a **generic** story on fishing," said Robin. Still, to make sure the journalists didn't see anything they weren't supposed to see, the government sent chaperones with them. "Four **government minders** were assigned to escort us wherever we went," said Robin.

As the officials brought her colleagues around the island, Robin managed to sneak off on her own. Once she was alone, Robin was able to speak to people she would not have seen if the government officials were at her side. She received her first tip from **prostitutes** who told her that many of their clients were Burmese fishermen.

This was the evidence the reporters had been looking for. It proved the workers were there. But Robin couldn't communicate with the men because she didn't speak their language. She arranged for Burmese-speaking AP reporter Esther Htusan to join her on the island. After Esther arrived, Robin explains, doors began to open. Once the enslaved men knew the women were reporters, they followed them everywhere. They were desperate to get their stories heard.

The men said they were trapped in Benjina. They'd been beaten, starved, barely paid, and kept from their homes and families— for decades in some cases.

They said the captains on their fishing boats forced them to drink unclean water and work 20- to 22-hour shifts with no days off. Almost all said they were kicked, whipped with **toxic** stingray tails or otherwise beaten if they complained or tried to rest. They were paid little or nothing, as they hauled in heavy nets with squid, shrimp, snapper, grouper and other fish.

From "Slaves may have caught the fish you bought," Associated Press investigation, March 2015

Robin and Esther's experience in Benjina illustrates the importance of journalists going to the site of a story. In person, they see things and gather information they could never find by scanning the Internet, official documents, or **databases**.

Over the next few days, Esther and Robin spoke to about 40 men, saw workers locked in cages, and visited a graveyard filled with dead fishermen. These men had been buried under false names to hide their identities. Before long, though, the reporters' investigation put them in danger. They were no longer safe on the island. As Robin describes in an interview, the fishing company officials had figured out what was going on. They warned the reporters to stay away.

On their last night in Benjina, Robin and Esther took a boat ride into the harbor to film workers transferring fish from **trawlers**, or fishing vessels, to a giant cargo ship. When workers inside the boats realized Esther spoke their language, they called out to her, pleading for help. They told the same stories of abuse and captivity.

Company officials in a speedboat also spotted Robin and Esther in the harbor. They chased the reporters, threatening to ram their tiny boat. Fortunately, when they realized Robin was foreign, they backed off. But Robin and Esther knew the fishing companies didn't want them there. They had made it clear that the reporters were at risk if they stayed on the island. Robin and Esther left Benjina the following morning.

Despite the safety risks they faced, the reporters did not give up their investigation. They felt a sense of responsibility to help the enslaved men (below). This sense of responsibility—to speak for people who otherwise would not be heard—is common to most investigative journalists.

Seafood goes through many steps, such as being sorted by workers at a shipping port (above), before it gets to a grocery store. It was challenging for the reporters to track where the slave-caught seafood ended up.

FROM SLAVE SHIPS TO AMERICAN MARKETS

Investigative journalists must prove the facts of their stories before they can publish them. By now, Robin and Esther believed that at least some of the seafood caught by slaves in Benjina was headed for the United States. The only way to prove it was to follow the seafood across the ocean.

After leaving the island, the reporters used an online satellite tracking service to monitor the seafood-filled ship's journey from Indonesia to Thailand.

Robin and Margie met the ship in Thailand when it arrived two weeks later.

Technology may have helped them follow the ship across the ocean, but for the next stage of the investigation, the women used old-fashioned stakeout techniques—again putting themselves in great danger.

They were warned to stay away from the ships. Armed guards patrolled the area. But Robin and Margie needed to know where the seafood was headed. The only way they could do this was to see it for themselves.

At great personal risk, they spent four nights in the back of a small truck hidden behind a wall. Through tinted windows, they observed seafood being dumped into trucks. Then they followed the trucks to processing plants, where seafood is inspected, sorted, and prepared for transportation to other locations, where eventually the seafood is sold and eaten. There, Robin and Margie watched the slave-caught seafood being mixed with other seafood and loaded onto cargo ships. The journalists documented everything they witnessed, including the names of the shipping companies that bought the seafood and sent it overseas.

Projects of this size are almost always team efforts. At this point, a fourth Associated Press reporter, Martha Mendoza, stepped into the investigation.

Based in the United States, she tracked the seafood-filled ships Robin and Margie had observed leaving Thailand. She searched **customs records** and business databases to find out which American companies bought the slave-caught seafood.

To be absolutely sure she had identified the correct businesses, she cross-checked and double-checked shipping dates, destinations, and the types of seafood on the boats. She even visited supermarkets to read frozen seafood labels, to prove the fish caught by Benjina slaves was being sold in the United States. It wasn't glamorous work, and it took months. "But eventually, the puzzle came together," said Martha. After weeks of tracking the ships, she could prove that seafood from Benjina was being supplied to supermarkets and restaurants in every American state.

*The team of reporters tracked shipping containers that they knew contained slave-caught seafood. Eventually, reporter Martha Mendoza could prove that the food was sold at "thousands of **outlets**" in the United States.*

*Shipping **port** in Bangkok, Thailand*

She even discovered that certain brands of pet food contained slave-caught fish.

Investigative journalists must report on all sides of a story, to give everyone involved a voice. Martha's next step, then, was to approach representatives of the companies she now knew were importing slave-caught seafood. None of the people she contacted would agree to be interviewed, but they all sent written statements making it clear they opposed the type of abuse the Associated Press reporters had uncovered.

Southeast Asian fish boats and processing plants keep poor records. They should document such things as when and where seafood is caught, where it is processed, and where it is headed. But they don't. The captains and companies are secretive.

Corrupt officials are involved. Fishing shipments are mixed together, making it almost impossible to know exactly where every fish comes from.

Because of these factors, many of the American fish companies contacted by the AP reporters may not have known some of the fish they bought was caught by slaves. Likewise, Indonesian government officials said they believed slavery was a problem of the past—they didn't realize it was still going on in their country.

They found out the truth in March 2015. That's when Robin, Margie, Esther, and Martha published their first seafood slavery story. Titled "Slaves may have caught the fish you bought," the story was published on the Associated Press website on March 25.

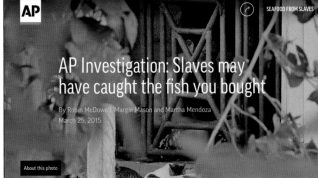

Newspapers, websites, TV, and radio stations around the world also picked up, or spread, the seafood slavery story. It received widespread attention.

AP SEAFOOD FROM SLAVES

AP Investigation: Slaves may have caught the fish you bought

By Robin McDowell, Margie Mason and Martha Mendoza
March 25, 2015

About this photo

BENJINA, Indonesia — The Burmese slaves sat on the floor and stared through the rusty bars of their locked cage, hidden on a tiny tropical island thousands of miles from home.

Just a few yards away, other workers loaded cargo ships with slave-caught seafood that clouds the supply networks of major supermarkets, restaurants and even pet stores in the United States.

But the eight imprisoned men were considered flight risks — laborers who

CHANGE-MAKING JOURNALISM

Before they released their story to the public, the group of AP investigative reporters took steps to ensure the safety of the men they had photographed and interviewed. They knew these men might be harmed for daring to speak out. They arranged for a human rights organization to rescue the men in question two weeks before the story ran.

A week after the story was published, a group of Indonesian government officials visited Benjina. Robin went with them.

The officials were "furious" when they saw what was happening on the island. Immediately, they offered to take with them anyone who wanted to go home. Word spread quickly. "People came in from places they'd been hiding—in the woods, behind the factory, or up in the hills," said Robin. Margie describes having tears in her eyes when she heard the good news from Robin. "It was a remarkable feeling to know that we had done this," she said. That day, 320 men left Benjina. Robin and Margie wrote an article about the spur-of-the-moment rescue operation early in April 2015.

PROTECTING SOURCES

Journalists rely on sources to learn information and receive tips. In many situations, however, it is dangerous for sources to talk to journalists. They may be targets for mistreatment by the people they are speaking against.

In the case of the Seafood Slavery story, many of the sources were slaves. These men provided information about the criminal activities of fishing boat captains and fishing company officials—people who didn't want the information made public.

When criminal activity is involved, people who speak up risk being harmed by the criminals. In such situations, sources may be afraid to talk to reporters. Or they may talk, but they don't allow their names to be used.

The Associated Press reporters who covered the Seafood Slavery story knew the slaves who spoke up could be harmed for sharing their experiences. Because of this, the journalists made sure the men were rescued—and safe—before the story was made public.

Over the next eight months, Robin, Margie, Esther, and Martha produced eight more stories and videos based on their investigation. In the end, more than 2,000 slaves were rescued. A number of Thai fishing boat captains and other abusers went to prison. Fishing boats were seized and businesses shut down. **Class action lawsuits** were filed. International seafood companies promised to change. Members of the public boycotted, or refused to buy, certain types of seafood. The United Nations, European Union, and United States launched investigations and threatened to ban Thai seafood unless the industry stopped human rights abuses.

The four AP reporters earned many journalism awards, including the prestigious Pulitzer Prize, for their Seafood Slavery series. In 2016, they published a book version of the investigative project titled *Fishermen Slaves: Human Trafficking and the Seafood We Eat*. All four reporters continue to work for Associated Press—Margie and Esther in Southeast Asia, Robin in Minnesota, and Martha in California.

Some human rights abuses are open secrets, and society tends to just accept them. Don't. As journalists, we can take an open secret and make people see it for what it really is. It's tough and can be emotionally exhausting, but it's so important not to give up even when you're told it's impossible. This project is proof that journalism can make a difference and truly give voice to those who are invisible.

Martha Mendoza, 2016

"BREATHLESS AND BURDENED"

WHO	American coal companies
WHAT	Denied medical benefits to workers who got sick on the job
WHEN	Late-1960s to 2012
WHERE	Virginia, West Virginia, Maryland
WHY	For profit
HOW	Hired doctors and lawyers to deliberately hide and misinterpret evidence

Many people believe human rights abuse is something that happens only in the world's poorest nations. Unfortunately, that's not the case. People around the world are capable of treating their fellow humans badly. Reporter Chris Hamby of The Center for Public Integrity discovered one such situation in the southeastern United States in 2013. The good news is that investigative reporters around the globe—journalists like Chris—work hard to bring these human rights violations into the public eye.

These investigations are never easy. People who abuse others do their best to cover it up by hiding the evidence.

Investigative journalists take great risks to dig up the proof they need to tell these stories. Sometimes, it can be almost too overwhelming to tackle.

Chris admits that, when he first discovered his award-winning story in 2013, he tried to ignore it. At the time, he was in the midst of another project. He was researching the return of black lung disease in coal miners in West Virginia.

Black lung disease is caused by inhaling coal dust. The dust builds up in the lungs, leading to scarring, coughing, difficulty breathing, and a variety of lung diseases. Many people eventually die from the illness.

Health benefits help pay for medications and medical care for workers. They also pay a salary to employees who are too sick to work. Because the miners had become sick on the job, they believed their employers would help them.

Rules were put in place about 50 years ago to protect miners from dust exposure and reduce the risk of developing black lung. But early in the 2000s, researchers discovered the disease was making a comeback.

This was the story on which Chris was working when he heard that coal-mining companies were denying health benefits to coal miners who suffered from the disease. To make sure they did not have to pay for the health benefits, the companies hired doctors and lawyers to misinterpret and hide evidence of black lung disease.

Chris heard stories like this over and over again. He knew that tackling this new story would be difficult. He was up against huge corporations with highly paid lawyers. "But the stories of sick miners being denied benefits kept coming," he said. In the end, no matter how big and complicated this story promised to be, Chris knew he couldn't ignore it. These miners needed help, and he was in a position to give them that help.

There are many reasons investigative journalists take on the stories they do. For many—especially those reporting on human rights issues—it's often a matter of doing the right thing. In this case, Chris couldn't let this wrongdoing go unreported. His personal commitment to truth and fairness wouldn't let him walk away.

In fall 2012, after he'd finished his first black lung investigation, Chris began digging into this new story.

DIGGING INTO THE INVESTIGATION

The goal of any investigative journalism project is to answer a question, or a series of questions.

Chris Hamby began his investigation into the lack of medical benefits for black lung victims with two questions: "Were significant numbers of sick and dying miners really being wrongfully denied benefits? And if so, how could this be happening?" Chris had heard many stories from miners, but he had to find out for himself if they were true. Good investigative journalists **verify** every fact and piece of information that comes their way. It took Chris a year to unravel the answers to his questions.

First, he contacted John Cline, a lawyer he'd met while writing his first black lung story. Making connections with experts is an important part of any investigative journalism project.

John knew many miners with black lung disease—and he knew that many of them had been denied benefits.

To confirm John's information, Chris reviewed online documents from the federal Labor Department. Public documents are often one of the first stops for investigative journalists. These are government or legal documents that citizens have a right to read. They include everything from police statements to lists of property owners in a town. Public documents contain a lot of information, if the reporter knows where to look.

The documents Chris reviewed were judges' **rulings** on coal miners' requests for health benefits. The documents showed that, over a period of about 10 years, 85 percent of miners with black lung disease had been denied benefits. Chris now had the answer to his first question: it was true that significant numbers of sick miners were being denied benefits.

Chris's second question, "How could this be happening?" was a lot harder to answer. From the public documents, he learned that judges usually sided with coal companies in denying health benefits to miners. Chris wondered why that was the case. Again, the lawyer, John Cline, had valuable information for Chris.

John had once helped a miner in his efforts to get health benefits. He gave Chris the case file that documented that miner's story. It contained shocking information about why the miner had been denied benefits: The coal company had hired expensive lawyers to represent it in court and had certain doctors review and give their opinions on medical tests. These legal and medical experts then deliberately hid evidence about the miner's health problems to make sure the miner wouldn't get any money.

John said this same thing had happened to other miners and their lawyers—and the complicated legal and health benefits systems allowed it to continue happening.

The opinions of doctors often swayed the judge's opinion in the black lung cases. Again and again, the coal companies hired the same doctors to give opinions in court. These doctors rarely found evidence of black lung when they reviewed medical tests.

The huge coal companies had the money to hire expensive teams of lawyers to argue their side. The coal miners were disadvantaged in court because of this.

With this information, Chris now knew he had a big story. But he needed evidence to show that lawyers and doctors deliberately twisted the truth, to mislead judges into denying health benefits. Chris wanted to prove that purposely denying health benefits was a pattern that affected thousands of sick miners. To do that, he needed to review more case files, like the one John had given him.

This posed a challenge. These particular legal documents were hidden behind **confidentiality laws**. The only records available to the public were the judges' final decisions that Chris had already reviewed online. These documents only recorded whether a judge had awarded or denied benefits. All other details were private and sealed from public view. But Chris didn't let that stop him.

> I want to tell stories that give power and say to the voiceless, and to hold the powerful entities— be they public or private—responsible.
>
> **Chris Hamby, 2014**

THE FACTS AND THE FACES

Investigative journalists are often blocked in their efforts to gather information. In many cases, certain people, governments, and businesses don't want particular details made public. Reporters frequently have to find other methods to get the facts they need.

In Chris's case, the public documents he already had contained names of miners. He tracked down as many of these men as he could. Some of the miners had died, so he contacted family members instead. He asked the miners and their families to waive, or give up, their rights to confidentiality so he could read the full case files. Almost everyone gave him written permission to do so. "Most felt that what had happened to them was wrong and wanted their stories told," he said.

Chris ended up with hundreds of thousands of pages of court documents. Some dated back 40 years. He read them all.

The job of an investigative journalist is often done in front of a computer, sitting at a desk, looking for certain bits of information. It takes time, commitment, and intense focus. But through this type of work, reporters often find the crucial evidence they need.

For months, Chris slowly read through stacks of court documents. To manage the masses of information they contained, he created a set of databases. He tracked medical evidence presented in court; he logged names of lawyers, judges, miners, and doctors involved in each case; he recorded dates, numbers, and timelines.

Next, Chris analyzed the data in his spreadsheets and found some surprising trends. He realized that coal companies **disputed** almost every benefits claim. If miners fought back, they'd be pulled into expensive legal battles that dragged on for years.

Chris also realized that the coal companies hired the same legal and medical experts in a huge number of the cases. The lawyers repeatedly hid evidence, twisted the truth, and dismissed scientific research that might help the miner. The doctors hired by the coal companies consistently said they saw no evidence of black lung disease on X-rays.

Chris and The Center for Public Integrity compared these doctors' findings with other doctors who looked at the X-rays. In most cases, many other doctors concluded that there was evidence of black lung.

Chris was particularly shocked to discover that one doctor from the world-renowned Johns Hopkins Medicine was involved in 1,500 of the miners' cases. In his opinion, not one of those miners had black lung disease. Working for the coal companies, this doctor shared this opinion in court over and over again. More than 800 miners lost their benefits cases because of this doctor's medical opinion.

The data in Chris's spreadsheets identified a system the lawyers had created to defeat miners' claims for medical benefits. The lawyers and medical specialists earned a lot of money for their roles in this system— and the miners got nothing.

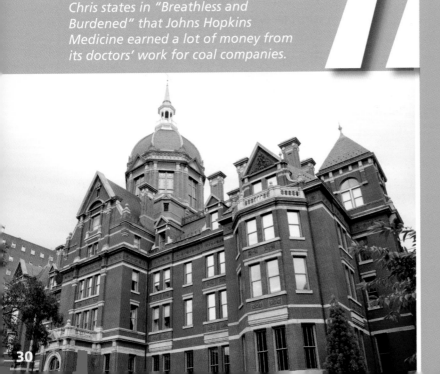

Chris states in "Breathless and Burdened" that Johns Hopkins Medicine earned a lot of money from its doctors' work for coal companies.

Sick and dying miners have been denied the modest benefits and affordable medical care that would allow them to survive and support their families.

Chris Hamby, "Breathless and Burdened," 2013

Chris documented the personal stories of suffering miners who had been denied benefits. These stories engage readers and catch their interest in the issue.

INTERVIEWS AND UNDERSTANDING

Journalists often interview experts to learn about an issue. They spend months or years learning complicated concepts and making sense of complex issues. Then, when they write the story, they need to simplify these concepts so that average readers can understand them. This is one of the most important parts of a journalist's job.

To help him understand the complex medical and legal details he read about during his research process, Chris interviewed "countless" legal and medical experts. His story uses visual elements, such as graphs, to explain some of the data he collected.

To further help readers understand— and relate to—complicated stories,

investigative journalists almost always add a personal point of view. They interview people directly affected by the issues in question to show the real-life impacts of the situation. Personal stories engage readers more easily than do facts and data—and engaging readers is a main goal of investigative journalism. Reporters want audiences to care about the issue so they'll take action to help change it.

For his black lung project, Chris focused on a few miners and their personal experiences. He interviewed the miners, their family members, and their doctors and lawyers. "These men allowed me into their homes and the most private corners of their lives," Chris wrote. "They were blunt, tough, kind and honest. I sat in their living rooms as they gasped for breath or inhaled oxygen from a tank."

CHANGE-MAKING JOURNALISM

After a year of documenting data, creating and analyzing spreadsheets, interviewing miners and medical and legal experts, Chris finally had enough evidence to publish his findings.

In the fall of 2013, he presented his three-part series, "Breathless and Burdened," on The Center for Public Integrity's website. He worked with reporters from *ABC News* Investigative Unit on the third part of the series. They produced a report on ABC's news's program, *Nightline*.

Chris's stories made an instant impact. The United States Congress immediately launched an investigation into the situation, and the Department of Labor made changes to the health benefits system. It also notified 1,100 miners that their benefits claims may have been wrongly denied because a particular doctor at Johns Hopkins Medicine had misdiagnosed them. Many of these miners filed a class action lawsuit against Johns Hopkins. That means they all got together to sue the institution. A judge disallowed the lawsuit in 2017.

In 2014, one woman was awarded medical benefits after her miner husband had died. The man had been denied benefits for nine years because the Johns Hopkins doctor said he didn't have black lung disease.

MULTIMEDIA INVESTIGATION

Often, an investigative journalism story appears in different media. "Breathless and Burdened," for example, was originally a text-based online project. But ABC Television worked with Chris to produce a video version of the story.

Stories are told in different ways in different media. That's partly because people prefer to get their information in different ways. It's also because each media type has certain strengths that allow it to highlight different story elements.

Print stories, for example, focus on written words and photographs and can include a lot of detail. Radio stories are told through sound and voices. People often listen to the radio or podcasts while doing other activities. Television stories rely on visual elements, and they are usually more fast-paced than audio or print versions of stories. That's because viewers want to see action, not just people talking.

Because of the specific focus of each media type, the same story may contain different information in each of the different formats.

But after he died, an **autopsy** showed that the miner did, in fact, suffer from black lung disease. At that point, the coal company stopped fighting the man's widow and started paying her a monthly sum of money.

Meanwhile, the doctor in question has since retired, and Johns Hopkins is no longer involved in any black lung cases.

Chris Hamby earned a Pulitzer Prize—and many other national journalism awards—for his "Breathless and Burdened" series. In 2014, he left The Center for Public Integrity. He now works in the investigative journalism unit of BuzzFeed News. In 2017, he was nominated for another Pulitzer Prize for his work on international crime.

HARVEST OF MISERY (COSECHA DE MISERIA)

WHO	Guatemalan children, as young as five
WHAT	Work on coffee plantations
WHEN	Reported in 2016
WHERE	Chiapas, Mexico
WHY	To help their families survive
HOW	Pick coffee berries and carry heavy sacks of coffee

Chocolate, cotton, sugar, tea. These are just some of the products harvested in faraway countries and imported to North America, where we enjoy them.

Sometimes, **consumers** are willing to pay a little extra for these items if they are ethically produced, or "fair trade." This means the products are gathered and processed in a way that does not harm workers—and that workers are paid a fair price for the products they produce.

Fair trade means, for example, that people who produce the chocolate are paid a good wage. It means laborers who pick tea leaves are treated well and work in healthy settings. It means cotton and sugar are farmed and processed in ways that don't harm the environment.

Products that meet these conditions are permitted to bear labels identifying them as fair trade. These labels tell consumers that inspectors have visited the farms or facilities that produced the items, and that those inspectors agree the items are ethically produced.

People who buy such products can feel good that their purchases are supporting healthy workers, workplaces, and the environment.
Or can they?

This was the question a group of television investigative journalists asked in 2015. The answer they found was disturbing.

The reporters focused their investigation on one of the world's most sought-after products—coffee. They traveled to Mexico, where there are many coffee plantations. They discovered that, when it came to certain brands, the fair trade label couldn't be trusted. Reporter John Carlos Frey described that the fair trade label is designed only to make consumers feel good—not to ensure that workers are safe or paid fairly.

He and his colleagues uncovered a "hidden truth" behind some so-called fair trade coffee labels—child labor.

THE COST OF A CUP OF COFFEE

Coffee is big business. It earns $80 billion a year for companies around the world. Coffee beans pass through many hands before they reach the consumer. First, farmers plant the coffee crop. Next, workers on plantations pick the beans. The beans are dried, milled to remove husks, and sorted in a processing facility.

Most coffee beans are exported from the countries that produce them to coffee companies in North America and Europe. There, the beans are roasted, packaged, and sold. Some coffee is sold as beans. Some coffee is ground before it is sold.

A SECRET LABOR FORCE

In 2015, two American television networks banded together to investigate the coffee industry in Mexico. The English-language Weather Channel and Spanish-language Telemundo had worked together in the past. In 2014, they'd produced an Emmy Award-winning documentary about migrant workers.

Investigative journalism projects always answer questions. Sometimes, though, they also raise new questions. That's what happened in this case.

While working on their first co-production, the journalists heard complaints about the working conditions in coffee plantations in southern Mexico, near the border of Guatemala.

They decided to join forces again to investigate. Reporters John Carlos Frey and Monica Villamizar took the lead on the project.

After months of planning, advance research, and organization, John Carlos and Monica flew to Chiapas, the southernmost state in Mexico. Half of Mexico's coffee crop comes from this region, and some of the biggest American coffee brands buy beans there.

The journalists' goal was to track the coffee from where it is grown in Chiapas to the big-name American companies that sell it. They also wanted to know whether consumers can trust product labels that promise that coffee is grown on organic farms where workers are treated fairly.

Chiapas is a state in southern Mexico. It borders Guatemala.

SHARING COSTS, SHARING NEWS

Investigative journalism is expensive. It can take months or years to pull together a well-researched report. In addition to journalists, it can involve editors, fact-checkers, photographers, videographers, specialized researchers, data analysts, and other team members. It can also involve expensive travel and equipment.

Because of this, media outlets sometimes join together to produce investigative journalism pieces—and to share the costs.

By traveling to witness the plantations, the reporters quickly confirmed that the rumors of poor living conditions for coffee workers in Chiapas were true.

THE STORY CHANGES

Sometimes, investigative journalists have an idea about where their stories will take them. At other times, stories unravel in completely unexpected ways.

For this story, John Carlos, Monica, and their crew planned to visit a number of coffee plantations. At the first one they came across, they discovered "horrendous" living conditions for coffee workers. The farm manager demanded they leave, so the journalists continued along

the hillside road. The journalists had expected to see workers living in dismal housing. Rumors about poor working conditions were what brought them to Chiapas.

Within minutes of leaving the first farm, they happened upon something they never expected to see—children lugging huge sacks of coffee berries. They were stunned. They stopped the car, jumped out, and started filming the parade of kids. Although it is against Mexican law for children under 15 to work, they found "an **assembly line** of the underaged," said John Carlos.

John Carlos and Monica immediately changed the focus of their investigation. They knew child labor was a major story that needed to be covered.

They followed a group of kids up a narrow hillside path. In the bushes, they found more children, some as young as five, picking coffee berries. They met a woman named Amalia and her eight kids. They were from Guatemala, just across the border from Chiapas. The whole family was picking and hauling coffee berries.

"The money is too little, but we have to keep going because we have no choice," said Amalia. "In Guatemala, there's no food unless you go out to earn money, so that's what we do."

Every year, from October to March, about 30,000 workers come to Chiapas from Guatemala for the coffee harvest. Parents can't leave their children behind, so they bring them along. If the children help with the harvest, families earn more money.

John Carlos and Monica spent several days in Chiapas, filming, talking to workers and farmers, and gathering information. Before they left the area, they also visited the local department of labor and a human rights organization. They wanted to make sure they heard all sides of the story. But neither office would answer their questions about child labor on the coffee plantations. People often don't want to, or are not permitted to, talk to journalists.

Children often carry bags that weigh up to 100 pounds (45 kg). This may harm their growth and cause spinal damage. Working in the bright Sun for many hours a day can damage children's eyes, leading to vision problems later in life.

They are often worried that they could suffer consequences, such as being fired, if they tell journalists any information.

Investigative journalists must have evidence to prove their research is true before they can present it to the public. They have the responsibility to prove any claims they make in the stories they write. John Carlos and Monica knew that they needed to prove that consumers in other parts of the world were buying coffee beans that had been picked from farms that used child labor. So before leaving Mexico, John Carlos and Monica made sure to record— with a GPS—the exact locations

where they had photographed and videotaped children working in Chiapas.

Once they were back in the United States, they located the GPS coordinates on maps, then used public records to identify the farms that allowed child labor.

This showed them who owned those farms. The next step was to track the sales of coffee beans picked at those farms to discover where they ended up in the world. Experts in Chiapas had told them it was "likely that coffee picked by kids will end up in the United States."

"The plantation owner isn't the one who makes them work, and neither is the government. The decision to allow children to work is made by the parents. Since they find themselves living in extreme poverty, parents allow this as a necessary evil."

Jorge Ausencio Aguilar, former priest, now works with small coffee companies

The reality for many families working on the farms is that all family members, including children, must work to make money to survive.

FAIR · TRADE

FAIR TRADE. NOT FREE TRADE

For coffee to be guaranteed fair trade, the farms where it comes from need to be inspected regularly. The reporters found this is not the case.

TRACING THE COFFEE TRAIL

In February 2016, another member of the investigative team, producer Marcus Stern, visited Chiapas. An important part of any journalism project is to get all sides of a story. In this case, Marcus interviewed local landowners and Mexico-based coffee companies.

Most of the officials they spoke to knew children worked with their parents picking coffee. In fact, many of the coffee company representatives had worked the farms with their own parents when they were children. Still, the coffee companies did their best to avoid farms that employ children. "But we can't control everything," one representative explained.

The reporters learned that coffee companies don't inspect and certify plantations themselves. They trust specialized organizations to do it for them. These organizations use a complicated mathematical formula to determine how many farms get inspected. It's not many. For example, of 5,144 farms in a group that includes the Chiapas area, 36 are inspected every three years. "The vast, vast, vast, vast majority go uninspected," said Marcus. "That means the chance that an actual inspector verified the coffee you're buying is next to zero," added John Carlos. It also means that some of the fair trade labels on the big-name coffee brands Americans buy are mostly meaningless. The fair trade certification is supposed to guarantee that, among other things, child labor is not involved in the production of the coffee. As these investigative reporters discovered, it doesn't.

Back in the United States, the reporters called all the major coffee companies that buy beans in Chiapas. They wanted to ask them whether they knew children were working on the farms that supply their coffee. None would speak to reporters.

CHANGE-MAKING JOURNALISM

In April 2016, John Carlos, Monica, and their crew returned to Chiapas for a third visit. This time, they saw no children. The harvest had ended in March, so the workers and their families had returned to Guatemala. They will return in October for the next harvest.

It took the television journalists almost a year to gather enough evidence to produce their stories. In July 2016, Telemundo presented a 45-minute Spanish-language documentary entitled *Cosecha de Miseria* ("Harvest of Misery"). Six months later, The Weather Channel produced an English-language multimedia version of the project. *The Source* is an online text and video presentation that features photos, maps, and links to other information.

After the group of journalists first visited Chiapas, Mexican police **raided** one of the farms. They found 50 families with children working there. Although the farm was closed temporarily to investigate, the officials reopened the farm after they determined the children had not been mistreated.

Though real consequences for the farms have not resulted, the documentary raised awareness about the child labor issue and informed consumers in North America that the fair trade label they trust is not always truthful.

Today, John Carlos Frey, Monica Villamizar, and Marcus Stern continue to work as independent investigative journalists.

HOME | ABOUT

THE SOURCE

The human cost hidden within a cup of coffee.

An Investigation by The Weather Channel and *Telemundo*

READ

Cosecha de Miseria won a 2017 Emmy Award for Outstanding Investigative Journalism In Spanish.

Everyone in the coffee belt in Chiapas knows this is how the system works. That's the secret. The labor laws, the certifications, the feel-good campaigns—they're **window dressing** meant to make us feel good about what we're buying. The only people who don't understand this reality are us consumers.

John Carlos Frey,
The Source, 2017

CONCLUSION

Investigative journalists around the globe present stories the world might otherwise never hear. They take months, or even years, to gather the evidence they need to publish these stories. They work in every media format—video, audio, photographs, text, even graphic novels. They also work in a variety of different subject areas.

Whether they produce projects about health care, business, human rights, or other fields, investigative journalists aim to present truths, highlight hidden problems, and engage audiences in issues that matter.

John Carlos Frey, Monica Villamizar, and Marcus Stern, for example, showed consumers that they couldn't always trust the product labels they read. This team of journalists also gave voice to desperate families and children who work hard to harvest coffee for very little money.

Human rights investigative journalists, perhaps more than any others, work to raise awareness about

The work of investigative journalists helps others learn about the issues affecting our world. It can raise public awareness and lead to social change.

mistreatment of people around the world. The four reporters from the Associated Press, for example, showed that slaves might have caught the seafood in restaurants and grocery stores around the world. They proved that the men had suffered so others could make a profit.

Investigative journalists seek to tell readers and viewers about secrets that should be out in the open, powerful people who abuse their positions, and systems that fail the people they're meant to help.

Chris Hamby, for example, discovered that wealthy coal mining companies deliberately cheated sick and dying employees out of the income they deserved.

Investigative journalists are driven by their natural curiosity, the courage to seek information others want hidden, and a keen sense of right and wrong. Their work often earns awards, honor, and respect. Perhaps more importantly, it can also lead to improvement for human rights around the world.

BIBLIOGRAPHY

CHAPTER 1

McDowell, Robin, Margie Mason and Martha Mendoza. "Slaves may have caught the fish you bought." Associated Press, March 25, 2015. https://bit.ly/1T1TEwV

"Investigative Journalism." UNESCO. https://bit.ly/2Pc6ERP

CHAPTER 2

Hare, Kristen. "How the AP busted an international seafood slavery racket." Poynter Institute, March 30, 2016. https://bit.ly/2MWuljv

Indonesia Expat. "Margie Mason, Pulitzer Prize Winning Journalist." Indonesia Expat, November 20, 2017. https://bit.ly/2PHvkCA

McDowell, Robin, Margie Mason, Martha Mendoza, and Esther Htusan. "Slaves may have caught the fish you bought." The Associated Press, March 25, 2015. https://bit.ly/1T1TEwV

Mendoza, Martha, Robin McDowell, Margie Mason, Esther Htusan. *Fishermen Slaves: Human Trafficking and the Seafood We Eat.* AP Editions, New York, New York, 2016. www.ap.org/books/fishermen-slaves/index.html

Niland, Olivia. "2016 Selden Ring Award ceremony honors Associated Press' 'Seafood from Slaves'" USC Annenberg School for Communication and Journalism, 2017. https://bit.ly/2wveRJb

Shinneman, Shawn. *The Story that Freed Hundreds of Slaves*. IRE Radio, 2015. https://bit.ly/2PG7Z4l

CHAPTER 3

Hamby, Chris. "Behind the story: 'Breathless and Burdened.'" The Center for Public Integrity, May 19, 2014. https://bit.ly/P3beSs

Hamby, Chris. "Coal industry's go-to law firm withheld evidence of black lung, at expense of sick miners." The Center for Public Integrity, October 29, 2013. https://bit.ly/2tytyJ8

Simone, Scott. "How I Got the Story: Breathless and Burdened." The Contently Foundation, 2014. https://bit.ly/2LwLlYT

The Center for Public Integrity. "Center wins first Pulitzer Prize." The Center for Public Integrity, May 19, 2014. https://bit.ly/2oe7FNR

CHAPTER 4

Noticias Telemundo. *Cosecha de Miseria*. Noticias Telemundo YouTube Channel, December 19, 2016. https://bit.ly/2MVJP7m

Stern, Marcus, et al. "The Source: The human cost hidden within a cup of coffee." The Weather Channel, January 19, 2017. https://features.weather.com/thesource

LEARNING MORE

BOOKS

Bausum, Ann. *Muckrakers: How Ida Tarbell, Upton Sinclair, and Lincoln Steffens Helped Expose Scandal, Inspire Reform, and Invent Investigative Journalism*. National Geographic Children's Books, 2007.

Mendoza, Martha, Robin McDowell, Margie Mason, Esther Htusan, and the Associated Press. *Fishermen Slaves: Human Trafficking and the Seafood We Eat*. AP Editions, 2016.

Muñoz Ryan, Pam. *Esperanza Rising*. Scholastic Inc., 2000.

WEBSITES

Fair Trade USA is a website devoted to raising awareness about fair trade products. This page, "Why Fair Trade?," offers definitions and links to stories related to fair trade around the world.
www.fairtradecertified.org/why-fair-trade

The Open School of Journalism's web page section on dual expertise describes the skills required for creating different types of stories.
www.openschoolofjournalism.com/ resources/journalism-education/ dual-expertise

This National Coffee Association website will tell you everything you need to know about coffee. Follow the 10 steps that detail how coffee is processed from start to finish.
www.ncausa.org/About-Coffee/ 10-Steps-from-Seed-to-Cup

LINKS TO ARTICLES IN THIS BOOK

Chapter 1–2

Mendoza, Martha, Robin McDowell, Margie Mason and Esther Htusan. "Seafood from Slaves." The Associated Press, 2016.
www.ap.org/explore/seafood-from-slaves

Chapter 3

Hamby, Chris. "Breathless and Burdened." The Center for Public Integrity, 2016.
www.publicintegrity.org/environment/ breathless-and-burdened

Chapter 4

Stern, Marcus, et al. "The Source: The human cost hidden within a cup of coffee." The Weather Channel, January 19, 2017.
https://features.weather.com/thesource

Noticias Telemundo. *Cosecha de Miseria*. Noticias Telemundo YouTube Channel, December 19, 2016.
https://bit.ly/2MVJP7m

GLOSSARY

abused Treated with cruelty or violence

activists People who take action to promote change

assembly line A phrase used to describe multiple workers and machines that do the same task repeatedly

autopsy A medical examination performed on a dead person

Burmese a person from the Southeast Asian country of Burma, also known as Myanmar

chaotic Confused, disordered, messy, out of control

class action lawsuits Lawsuits in which a group of people who suffered similar harm sue the defendant together, as a group

concealed Hidden

confidentiality laws Rules made by government that protect the privacy of one's personal information

consumers People who buys goods and services

conventional Traditional, regular, ordinary

corrupt Willing to act unethically or dishonestly for personal gain

customs records Documents that keep track of people, vehicles, and items moved across a border from one country to another

databases Collections of information that are organized in a way that it is easy to search, manage, and update

disputed Argued or fought over something

ethically Fairly, justly, or honorably

exploited Took advantage of

exporter A company that sells products or services to another country

fertilizers Chemical products spread on soil to help plants grow

follow-ups News stories inspired by a previous, related news story

generic Not specific

government minder someone who is assigned by the government to watch over foreign visitors

imported Brought in from another country

industry The making and selling of specific goods and services

inhumane Cruel, lacking compassion and kindness

LGBTQ spectrum People who do not identify as heterosexual or as having the gender identify assigned to them at birth; stands for lesbian, gay, bisexual, transgender, queer or questioning

migrant workers People who move from place to place (often to another country) to find seasonal work

networking Communicating with others to share information and contacts, as a way of reaching goals and furthering one's career

objectivity The quality of being unbiased, fair, neutral

outlet A news outlet is a company that publishes news and media

plantations Large farms where certain crops are grown

port A town, city, or harbor where ships load and unload goods

proactive Taking action, rather than waiting for something to happen

profit Money made by selling something after the cost of producing it has been paid

prostitutes People who engage in sexual activity in exchange for money

protest Publicly speak out against something

raided entered a place suddenly in a forceful way in order to look for something

rulings In court, decisions made by a judge

satellite Technology that orbits Earth to collect information

sources People, documents, videos, recordings, or other publications that provide information to a journalist

stakeouts Operations in which a location is secretly watched continuously for a period of time

toxic Poisonous

trawlers Fishing boats that catch fish by dragging a net through the water

United Nations An organization made up of 193 countries that works to promote world peace and human rights about the world

verify To confirm or prove something is true

vulnerable Easily hurt or harmed

window dressing To alter how something is viewed to make a positive impression

INDEX

ABOUT THE AUTHOR

Diane Dakers has been a print and broadcast journalist since 1991. She specializes in culture, science, and business reporting. She has also written 24 nonfiction and 3 fiction books for youth.